NATIONAL GEOGRAPHIC
School Publishing

Prehistoric Life

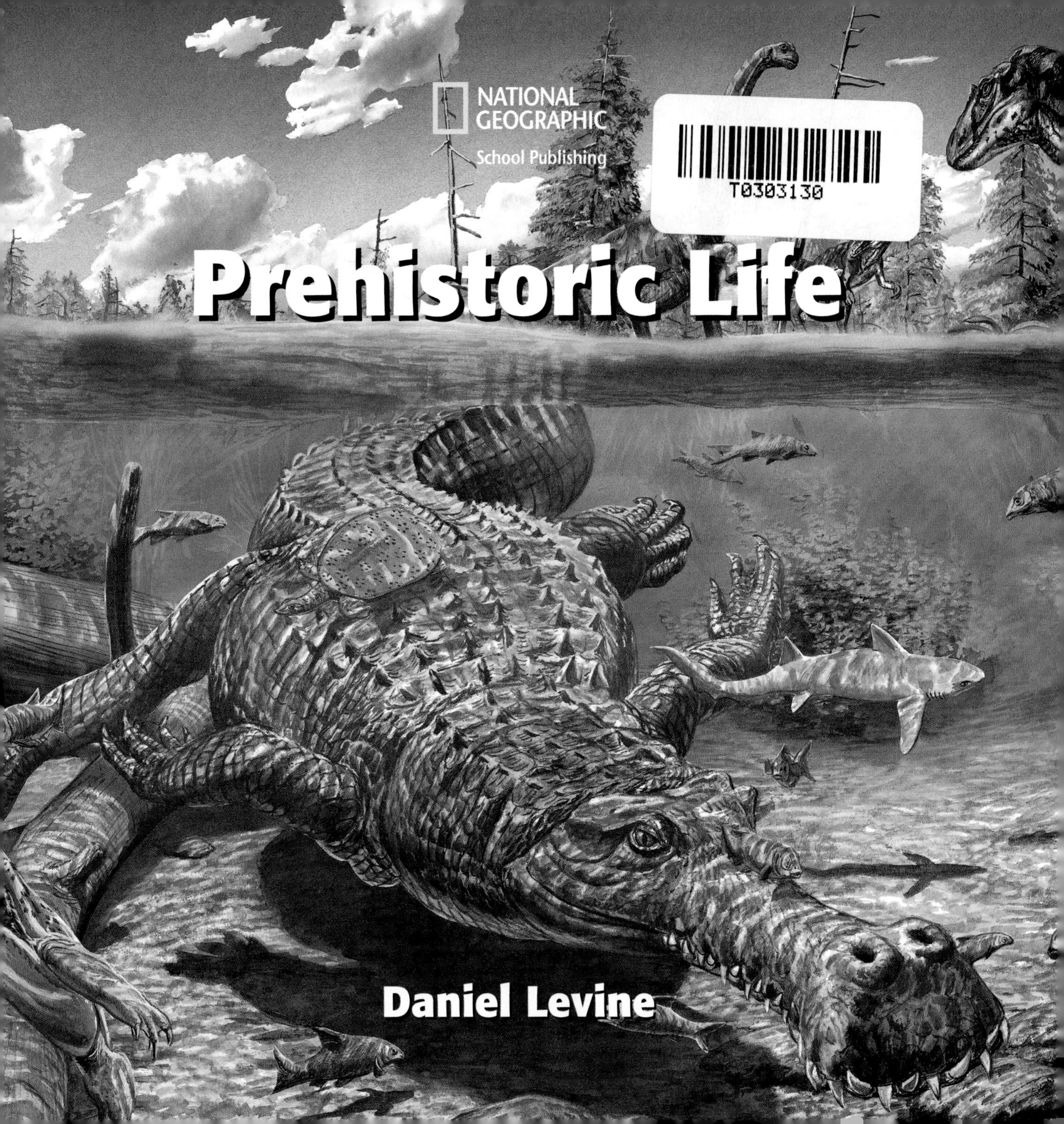

Daniel Levine

PICTURE CREDITS
Cover, 1, 4 (above), 4 (below), 5 (left above), 5 (left below), 5 (right), 6 (left), 6 (right), 7, 8 (above), 8 (below), 9 (above), 9 (below), 10, 11 (above), 11 (below), 13 (right), 14, 15 (left above), 15 (left below), 16, 18 (right below), 19 (above), 19 (below), Photolibrary.com; 2, 13 (left), 18 (above), 18 (left below), Getty Images; 12, James L. Amos/National Geographic Image Collection; 17 (above), Todd Gipstein/National Geographic Image Collection; 17 (below), Kurt Mutchler/National Geographic Image Collection; 15 (right), Ilya Naymushin/REUTERS/Picture Media.

Produced through the worldwide resources of the National Geographic Society, John M. Fahey, Jr., President and Chief Executive Officer; Gilbert M. Grosvenor, Chairman of the Board; Nina D. Hoffman, Executive Vice President and President, Books and Education Publishing Group.

PREPARED BY NATIONAL GEOGRAPHIC SCHOOL PUBLISHING
Steve Mico, Executive Vice President and Publisher, Children's Books and Education Publishing Group; Marianne Hiland, Editor in Chief; Lynnette Brent, Executive Editor; Michael Murphy and Barbara Wood, Senior Editors; Nicole Rouse, Editor; Bea Jackson, Design Director; David Dumo, Art Director; Shanin Glenn, Designer; Margaret Sidlosky, Illustrations Director; Matt Wascavage, Manager of Publishing Services; Sean Philpotts, Production Manager.

MANUFACTURING AND QUALITY MANAGEMENT
Christopher A. Liedel, Chief Financial Officer; Phillip L. Schlosser, Vice President; Clifton M. Brown III, Director.

BOOK DEVELOPMENT
Ibis for Kids Australia Pty Limited.

Published by the National Geographic Society
1145 17th Street, N.W.
Washington, D.C. 20036-4688

Product No. 4W1005057

ISBN-13: 978-1-4263-5053-5
ISBN-10: 1-4263-5053-8

2017 2016 2015
2 3 4 5 6 7 8 9 10 11 12 13 14 15

Printed in the U.S.A.

Contents

Think and Discuss

scientists

woolly mammoth in museum

What do you know about prehistoric life?
How do we learn about prehistoric life?

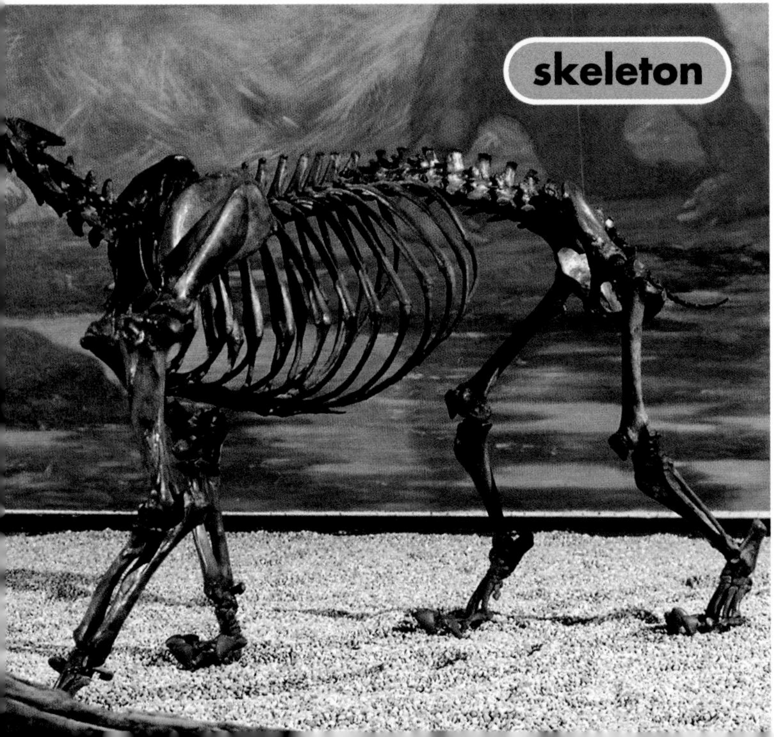

Life Long Ago

Prehistoric plants and animals lived on Earth long ago. Most prehistoric life died out, or became **extinct**, millions of years ago.

This prehistoric sea creature lived more than 570 million years ago.

Dinosaurs were prehistoric reptiles. They lived about 240 million years ago.

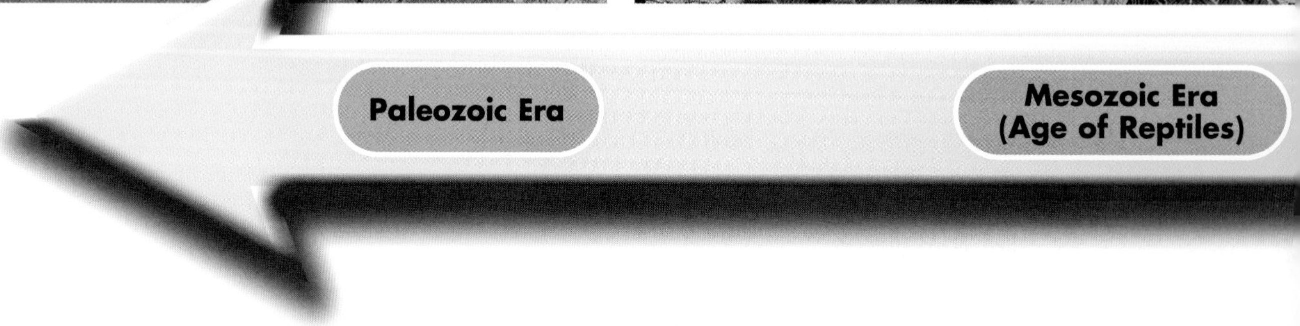

Mammoths were prehistoric mammals. They lived about 65 million years ago.

Cenozoic Era (Age of Mammals)

Prehistoric Relatives

Some plants and animals that exist today are related to prehistoric plants and animals.

This is an imprint, or mark, of a plant in a rock. It is from prehistoric times. Ferns like this one still grow today.

Crocodiles existed at the same time as the dinosaurs. Crocodiles today are smaller but look very similar.

Learning About Prehistoric Life

Some scientists are called **paleontologists**. Paleontologists study the **remains** of prehistoric plants and animals.

This paleontologist is brushing away soil from a dinosaur **skeleton**.

Paleontologists use many different kinds of tools.

These paleontologists are removing rock from a prehistoric skeleton.

Fossils

Remains of prehistoric life are called **fossils**. Some fossils look like pictures in rocks.

Scientists have found many plant fossils in rocks.

Scientists have found many animal fossils in rocks.

Fossils can also be imprints in rock. This fossil is a dinosaur footprint.

Some animal fossils are bones, eggs, or even whole creatures.

These insect fossils are in hardened tree sap.

These fossils are dinosaur eggs.

This plant fossil was found frozen in ice.

In 1997, a young boy found a woolly mammoth frozen in the ground. This model of a woolly mammoth is in a museum.

Picturing Prehistoric Life

Paleontologists put animal bones together to make skeletons. These skeletons help people make drawings and models of prehistoric animals.

This woolly mammoth skeleton is in a museum.

Dinosaur robots are sometimes used in movies and in museums.

Artists use plaster, clay, and other materials to build models of prehistoric creatures.

Use What You Learned

You might see all these things in a museum. Talk about these pictures.

dinosaur

extinct

fossil

paleontologist

prehistoric

remains

skeleton

Picture Glossary

dinosaur

fossil

paleontologist

skeleton